Perceptions

&

Perspectives

Your kindness is your strength
Your strength is your kindness

Scott Healy

Interior & Cover Layout: Pickawoowoo Publishing Group
Cover photo by John Collins, Pixabay.

A catalogue record for this
book is available from the
National Library of Australia

NATIONAL
LIBRARY
OF AUSTRALIA

978-0-646-82064-4 (Paperback)
978-0-646-82063-7 (Ebook)

Disclaimer
This book is not intended as a substitute for the medical advice of physicians directly or
indirectly for any technique as a treatment for mental or physical problems. You may consult
a physician in matters relating to your health in regards to any symptoms that may require
diagnosis or medical attention. The author's intention is to offer general information in support
of your journey for body, mind and energy wellbeing. The author assumes no responsibility
for your personal actions.

Facebook : Perceptions & Perspectives

*To all my friends and family who have
supported me throughout my life.
All the good times, all the bad times.
They are what made us all stronger.
They are what made our bonds closer.*

*Thank you from every part of
my heart and soul...*

Other People's Pain

is Not Mine to

Carry…

To Make them

Better

is My Journey

Table of Contents

Premise

During your reading of this book, there will be some writings about the dark times I went through quite a few years ago.

Often I thought they would destroy me.

Although, I am glad that I wrote everything down about how I was feeling, so I can share it with the people who feel they have no voice.

Through keeping my head above water, I came out the other side. Stronger and better than ever.

The dark times are what made me who I am today. They are a thing of the past. Positivity and hope are what rule my mind now.

I hope that anyone who is struggling on their path at the moment finds some solace in my words.

I understand how you feel, I do.

But there is always hope if you just keep putting one foot in front of the other....

I can only write words

I can only provide my opinions

*I can't change anything in
your life, only you can*

Scott Healy

About The Author

I've become highly aware of my empath state only in the last couple of years. I'm glad it came to me later in life.

It is natural to me. It feels normal.

It is exactly the person I always wanted to be. So therefore, I accept it with open arms.

My journey is to heal others.

But to do that, I first had to break myself back down to human basics, and very quickly build myself back up with the knowledge I have in my psyche.

Self healing is an art. It is something you slowly teach yourself, through tearing away the fabric of who you are as a human being.

Touching those nerves that make you scream with pain. The ones that make you cry.

But... Those tears aren't pain. They are healing.

Sometimes we cry when we are happy, and sometimes we cry when we are sad. Sometimes we cry because our soul feels broken.

Crying when you are broken is healing, because your soul has realised what has hurt you.

Always remember, your soul is your best friend, not your enemy. Treat it with respect, it's your eternal guide.

Show me the hand of someone who needs a leader, and I will teach them that the only leader they need is themselves.

All I ask from the universe is that my
words find the people who need them...

A Letter to My Angel On Earth

We often meet the people we trust the most, when we least expect it.

We shouldn't search for them. They arrive when we need them.

They help keep us grounded, and they trust us with all their hearts.

My protector. My guidance counsellor. My friend.

You tell me the brutal truth. You make me a better person.

Thank you for all your support. Thank you for just being you...

I know there is someone out there
who appreciates you for the person
you are.

But you always doubt the person
you are, so you try to be
someone that you think people
want you to be.

Don't pretend. Just be yourself.
The best version of you, is you...

Scott Healy

Philosophy

I will never understand how a person can judge another by the shade of their skin. It is something I will never understand.

Life is not about judging others, it is about our journey, and who we become as human beings in this incredible world.

We start our lives with a clean slate, and the moment we are born, we look for love and nurturing. The touch of our mother and the warmth of her breast.

We ultimately search for the love of another human being with whom we feel safe, and can love unconditionally.

Ever since humans found a way to care about each other, they have also found a way of hating someone because of the way they look. Not because of how they behave in society, or how they treat their fellow humans, but because of how they look.

We come from the same place, we all have a common thing that binds us. We are human beings who have red blood that runs beneath our skin.

No human being is better than the other. No skin colour is better than the other. We all eat the same, we all speak the same, and our sense of humour reaches across all languages.

We have a common goal of treating each other the way we want to be treated ourselves.

Despite the fact that there are people who try to put hate into our souls, humans are not born to hate.

Humans are born to be loving and caring.

Children are not born racist either. They treat each other the way they are treated.

A child doesn't see the colour of their friends' skin. They just see someone they can play with.

It is a parent that breeds hate into a child's life, and it is a parent that also breeds love.

Love is something that will never tear us apart, and we will fight to keep the people we love safe.

Life is a journey, and we only learn the truth when it is through.

That does not stop us from loving the people who are close to us, and being a decent human being in a world that seems so cruel sometimes.

Life is only cruel though if we allow it to be. Life is only judgmental when we let the hate of others cloud our own judgement.

If we keep our eyes open and look for the good that surrounds us, then the trees will always look green, the sky will always be blue, and no cloud will keep away the sunshine.

*Self esteem is the strongest attribute
you can ever have...*

*Without your self esteem,
you are a slave to others judgement.*

Scott Healy

The Most Important

The most important people in your life are the ones that hold you up high on their shoulders. The ones who don't judge you.

The ones who accept your faults.

The ones who look up to you, just like you look up to them.

Even though you may doubt yourself, there are people who believe in you more than they believe in themselves.

Believe in yourself as much as they do.

People are only lonely, because they are told by society that they need to have someone else in their life.

Freedom and happiness is achieved when you realise that you are happy within yourself.

Scott Healy

Awakenings

Most of the time, I'm just a normal human being, trying to make life simple and fun.

Sometimes I'm able to help people see life in a different perspective.

You don't need to know the meaning of life.

You don't need to have an awakening.

You just need to be a good person. A simple person.

The wonders of the universe may be overwhelming, and yes, they are...

How can you ponder the intricacies of the universe, when you can't understand yourself? The universe will look after itself, and it will continue to, long after we are all gone.

Be kind to yourself.

You are the one that has to live with yourself, so you may as well try and make it as comfortable as possible.

The one thing I can do, is give encouragement.

I have walked through hell myself. I know pain. I know the feeling of total worthlessness. I've walked that path.

I know what it's like to look death in the eye, and not care. It is a feeling I will forget, but always remember. It is there in the subconscious to know that it is not worth it.

I can't save the world, but I can give hope to the ones who understand pain.

You are ultimately the one in control of your life. You are the one that needs to be nice to yourself.

It's easier said than done... I know that. But it doesn't hurt to try one step at a time?

If part of my life involves making a few people smile, then it makes my life more worthwhile....

Love

I screamed your name,
Through all the pain,
But still you couldn't hear
This darkness can't go on forever,
My eyes are filled with tears

I never knew, I've never seen,
A life that can be real
It's you that makes me feel my soul,
I need your heart to heal

But you passed me by and never saw,
The person you could be
If only you had seen my eyes,
Our lives could be so free

Memories

The memories we have of the people we loved.

The memories we hold in our hearts.

The memories that are forever etched in our souls.

The memories that will never pass.

The more seeds that are planted into our minds by others, even if they are poisonous, will only grow as much as we allow them to.

Scott Healy

Sands of Time

The sun it shined so brightly
As our feet they touched the water
I held your hand so tightly
As your soul it gave me shelter

A smile that every angel
Could see from up above
I thought that I saw heaven
All my heart could feel was love

But another stone is another road
That winds a weary path
A road that leads to nowhere
When your heart it seems so far

Our souls are fragile, our minds are weak
My faith in life has waned
I only hope I find my heart
That's left me once again

Why did you cause all of this pain?
Where did your warm heart go?
How did you leave me all alone?
In a place I've never known

I can't forget, you left me here
The time it passes slow
The world it seems so dark,
I have to let you go

You chose your path, you walked away
Why did you seem so real?
I'll find myself, I'll live again,
The sands of time will heal.

No matter how far, or how fast you run,
you can never run away from your mind

Scott Healy

Personal Responsibility

*We are all guilty of not taking personal
responsibility for ourselves.*

*Sometimes we like to take the easy option out and rely
on others to solve our problems.*

The only person that is responsible for you is yourself.

*If you don't take that personal responsibility, then you
become reliant on society to make decisions for you.*

*If you allow society to make decisions for you, then you will never be
happy. You will be miserable.*

*Stand up for yourself
Make decisions for yourself
Make mistakes
Learn from them*

When you learn to rely on yourself, your whole life will change.

If you are your own worst enemy,
then everyone else will see you as
an enemy.

Scott Healy

Dear Father

To the father I never knew

The father who was not a father

I don't hate you. I feel sorry for you

I feel sorry for you because you never saw the man I have become

I haven't missed out on anything. You have.

You chose not to care

You chose to live your life the way you did

I chose to live mine better

My Real Father

I always wished I had a father
A father just like you
I wish we spent more time together
But you never really knew

I treated you so bad at times
But I hope I don't regret
I need to keep your memory
Always in my head

You taught me how to be a man
A man that's just like you
The man I have become today
Is all because of you

I wish that I had hugged you
I wish you could be here
We miss you oh so very much
But your heart is always near

You'll never be away from us
You're always in our hearts
A man like you is hard to find
We'll never be apart

I hope that you can see me
I hear your words so loud
I miss you more than words can say
I hope I make you proud

You can love and care about as many people as you want.... But the most important person is always yourself.

Scott Healy

Letter To Billie

Dear Billie,

Just like my little sister, your mother, I remember the first time I saw you.

I hope you keep this letter as you get older and remember that I always believe in you.

As you grow, you will make mistakes and you will learn from them. If you don't make mistakes, then you don't know how to become stronger.

I learnt a lot of lessons in my life. Some of them were really hard, and some of them were easy. The hardest ones were the ones that taught me who I am.

We may not get to spend a lot of time together, but when we do, I hope that you can cherish those times as much as I will. I hope that I help you become a better person. I hope that you choose to have good people in your life. I hope that you find someone that loves you as much as you love them.

The most important thing in life is to have people that love you for who you are, not who they want you to be.

Be crazy, be silly. Dance like an idiot. Say things that make you laugh at yourself, because you always need to laugh at yourself.

You have an amazing mum and dad. They are very important to me. Your mother is more amazing than you may ever know. Her strength is something that flows through our blood.

I wish you had the chance to meet your Grandfather. He was a beautiful soul.

Everyone loved him. He brought everyone together.

When he passed away, I heard the loudest clap of thunder I have ever heard. I knew it was him.

I drove home and cried the whole way.

Always question yourself.
Always question life.
No one is better than you.
You are also no better than anyone else.

*No one knows they have been lost
until they find themselves...*

Scott Healy

Love and Pain

There is nothing more painful than feeling your heart break.

For whatever reason it breaks, the feeling of your heart tearing apart and dropping away from your soul is indescribable.

It feels like you have lost a part of you, and you don't know whether you can replace that part again. How do you put back a part of your heart that you can't find?

Your heart will still do what it has to do, but the emotional part of it is something that can be so hard to find again.

Every time you give a part of it away, you take a chance. That part is always gone if you don't find what you are looking for.

Take a chance. Give your heart a chance to break. If you keep your heart locked away because you are afraid of it breaking, then you will never find what you are looking for...

Our peers are not our judges
You are your own judge...
Use your judgement wisely.

Scott Healy

The Different Paths

There are so many paths in front of us. There are warning signs that tell us not to enter on some of them. There are decisions our hearts make, and there are decisions our minds make.

Without these different paths, and right and wrong decisions, we will never grow and learn.

Sometimes we have to be completely lost. Without losing yourself, how can you find yourself? How can you learn and grow if you stay sheltered in your safe little haven?

The paths that have warning signs are often the ones that teach us the hardest lessons. The lessons that need to be felt. The lessons that tear apart your soul.

The lessons that also make you that little bit stronger when you find your way out of the darkness.

Surprise your mind

Do something it doesn't expect......

Scott Healy

People

The people you trusted. The people you believed were honest. The people who never had your best interests at heart, but had ulterior motives that suited their own purposes.

These people don't have pure souls. They only look for the next opportunity that will benefit their broken purpose in life. A purpose that serves nothing in humanity and their personal relationships.

For some of them it is "fight or flight", and these confused souls don't ever seem to find the right path. They do what they have to do to survive.

The other people in this equation are narcissistic, self-absorbed people.

As we grow older, we learn to rid our lives of people who do not enrich us. If we don't, then we continue to repeat the past.

> *Regrets are a curse that stop
> you from moving forward.*
>
> *Scott Healy*

When we judge others, we forget to look at ourselves.

When you are judging someone, you are really just looking in the mirror.

Scott Healy

Pain

When you first confront your pain,
it is going to feel like you are dying inside.

The rawness, the emotions.
Pain.
Anger.

The pain is not destroying you. It is surging a life force through you,
to teach you never to go back to whatever it is that caused the pain.

Pain and memories leave scars that teach you lessons.
Lessons you had to learn. Lessons that felt like they
would suffocate you...

Be patient.

Believe in yourself

*Until you understand hate, you
will never be able to control it...*

*Hate is an insidious disease that
only affects the person carrying it*

Scott Healy

You......

Only when I stopped searching for you did I find you.

When I saw your eyes, I could see through your soul. Like our souls had always been together through eternity.

Finally, we found each other again on this mortal earth.

Your arms feel like they have always been around me, but I never understood how much I missed them until our hearts were beating together.

Every second, every day felt like an eternity without you beside me. We all have our paths to walk, but my path has felt covered with loneliness, until you came back to me.

I have learnt lessons. I have learnt to be myself without you there. I have reached the lowest depths. I have felt the ecstasy of life. But nothing replaces the feeling of you being next to me.

I don't regret the time we spent apart. We both had to learn what life has to offer. We also needed to find our own way in this world before we could be together again.

I want to learn the rest of my lessons in life with you by my side.

It hurts to learn lessons alone and not have the comfort of your soul.

We have only just begun our new journey.

We have only just been born.

Hold my hand and let's take the rest of our journey together.

I hope that everything you have done in your life led you back to me.

I hope that you missed me while we were apart. I hope that you never let me go again.

I need to fall asleep next you every night. I need to see your eyes in the morning.

Humans...

Humans are such tortured creatures. The frailties we have. The pain we feel. The love that makes our heart ache.

With intelligence comes self-awareness.
With self-awareness comes doubt.
With doubt comes emotions.

Emotions are impossible to control, as much as we try.

Emotions are part of our soul. They are not a conscious thing.

Therefore, as much as people try to bury certain emotions, they will manifest themselves in a way that we don't want them to.

Anger that builds inside you.

Anger that can be taken out on someone completely undeserving of it.

Emotions are not something to be ignored. They must be dealt with.

Crying. Screaming alone.
Listening to music.
Walking on the beach.

Breathing deeply and slowly.
Time is a wonderful thing if you know how to use it.

Time does heal all wounds, even if there are scars left. Those scars are what teach us lessons, and make us better, stronger people.

When you start to control your mind, rather than letting it control you, you are capable of anything.

You can strive to be the best at your art, or you can strive for inner peace.

No matter what path you choose, it is a journey.

A journey of becoming more self-aware of who you are and where you belong in the universe.

Don't let the little things in life distract you from the goal you want for yourself as a human being....

Sometimes we have to walk through hell to get to heaven...

Scott Healy

Breathe

When I breathe, I feel everything that life has to offer.

It drowns me sometimes

I can't understand why I am so lost in this world.

I keep breathing ....

I wish that I never felt anything. It's easier.
I want to die, but I want to breathe

Life is an amazing thing, but sometimes I feel like I must exist to make sure that the people who care about me are happy.

Why should I pretend to be happy just to make others happy?

How can life be a happy place when you feel so lonely?

How can you be such a beautiful person inside, but you are left to hold your own heart?

Just a touch... Just a hand....

I want someone to feel my soul.

Just make me feel something.

What is it like to love someone?

To have them want nothing more than to kiss you.

Why do I have to live this life alone?

It's not fair.

But is life ever fair?

I want it to stop and let me be peaceful.

I am peaceful

But there is something missing

I'll just wander along...

You want to risk your life?

Make it a life you want to risk....

Scott Healy

Self-Worth

I was never sure if I had self-worth. I was never sure if I belonged in this world.

I always pushed myself away from people because I felt insecure. I felt different.

A few people in my life have changed how I think of myself, but I still have to be comfortable with who I am as a human being.

Maybe I am so damaged from my previous experiences with humans, that I have become lost in my own world.

I know that things will eventually get better. I am too strong and too smart not get through this. I know I will come out stronger...But when

Misery

There is comfort in misery. It means that you only have to take minimal responsibility for yourself, and hope that people feel sorry for you.

Happiness is a lot harder to find than misery.

We can find misery everywhere if we want.

Happiness sometimes feels like the pot at the end of the rainbow.

You can only find it if you stop looking for it.

Just because we perceive something,
does not mean that
perception is reality..

Scott Healy

My Torture

I get it. I truly get it. I'm like a square peg trying to fit in a round hole.

I try, I really do. Maybe I don't try enough, or maybe I try too hard. Maybe I'm just not meant to fit into this mortal world? Maybe this is my torture?

Even the people who love me don't get me. Sometimes I feel they just tolerate me.

Everything is an act. But I don't know how to act very well.

I don't like being around people. I don't like having to pretend that I do. But I feel compelled to interact with them.

Occasionally they make me smile and laugh. But it's only fleeting moments.

I like who I am. I like my mind.
I like my soul. I like my heart.

It takes a special person to understand me.

That is why I keep the people close to me close, even though it seems like I try to push them away...

Depression # 1

Depression twists your mind in a direction that you can never imagine.

All the alcohol and all the drugs in the world will never be strong enough....

Believe me, I have tried.

I am intelligent and eloquent.

Why doesn't anyone want to listen?

I have tried to talk to the people closest to me.

I have tried to give them an insight into how I am feeling.

I have tried to tell them that it is not just a tap on the shoulder, and everything will be alright.

It is something that takes control of the deepest parts of your mind.

It is like an invisible cancer.

I'm embarrassed and ashamed for not being able to pretend that everything is alright.

I find it hard to express emotions towards the people who mean the most to me.

Why can I hug a stranger. But I can't hold my mum in my arms like she is the most important person in the world?

It's not me that is afraid to talk

It is the voice inside my head that tells me to be quiet.

"Don't talk...

Shut up. . .

No one cares what you think..."

You try so hard to explain to yourself what is happening in your mind.

You trace back what has happened during the day, but it all becomes a blur.

Your mind just tells you that everything you do is wrong, and you should kill yourself.

Only the people who have felt this trauma can understand what I am saying.

My mind is sometimes consumed with suicide.

How will I do it?

How can I do it in the least painful way?

What happens when I die?

Will I end up in purgatory?

Will I be made to relive what I did to myself in the mortal world?

The darkness of depression is something that cannot be explained in words properly

I can only hope that one day I can be cured of this curse

If there is in fact a cure?

Philosophy is theoretical.
Listening to and understanding
someone is beyond that...

Scott Healy

Depression #2 Better

Life up until a couple of years ago was not always the happiest.

I'm not saying I have had a bad life, but quite often my mind has tried to tell me that it was.

I have fought depression most of my life. I don't normally mention it, because I have been able to just hold myself together, and have only relied on myself to get through it.

From my late teenage years to my early 40's, I have been to hell and back. But only in my own mind.

Anyone who has suffered depression knows what I am talking about.

But you only know you are suffering depression if you recognise it.

I recognised it, and I was well-aware of it during my 20's

I pushed it to the back of my mind like it was something I could deal with when I was ready.

Well, I didn't deal with it very well at times. I kept running away from it.

I treated my stepfather like he was the devil when I was a teenager.

I don't really have regrets, but I immensely regret the way I treated my stepfather when I was a teenager.

Thankfully, the last time I saw him before he passed away, I told him I was the happiest I had ever been (I thought I was anyway). He smiled at me. That was the last time I saw him.

I didn't realise how important he had been in my life until I couldn't talk to him anymore.

But this is not about missing someone, it is about depression, and how it can wreck your life if you allow it.

Depression is an insidious disease that can affect anyone. It is a chemical imbalance in the brain. It is not something that affects only the weak, it can affect anyone, whether you notice it or not.

There is not a time in life that people have not questioned themselves. But depression turns that question into a question that is hard to answer at times.

I have gone through times where I would close my front door and hope that the world would just go away and leave me alone. It never did, it was always outside the door, and as much as I resisted, it was something I had to face. Some of the worst times were just locking myself away and drinking for days on end.

If I really had to deal with people, I would go out and put on a fake smile. I would do what I needed to do, just so I could go home and forget that I went out.

To keep your head above water and make sure that you keep breathing is exhausting.

Because it is so exhausting, you lose the ability to have the energy to interact with other people. Even though you know you are fully capable of interacting, you have exhausted everything just trying to look after yourself and your mental state.

In your mind, you just want to take the easy option out, and that is suicide. I have sat on a window ledge, waiting to fall. You imagine how you would do it. You imagine if it would hurt. You don't think about anyone else, because you just want whatever pain you are feeling at the time to go away, and that pain can be excruciating.

I want anyone who reads this to know that it is not the end of the world when your brain feels like it is twisted in knots.

You are smarter than you know!

I am not trying to be a motivational speaker, I am trying to say that I know how you feel. It hurts, it makes you cry, and you don't know what wall to hit your head against!

Thankfully I am not in that place anymore, and depression is something that is hopefully in the past for me.

Depression is not something that is cured by someone patting you on the back and telling you everything is alright.

It is not about someone just having a bad day. It needs to be dealt with by professionals. It doesn't mean you need to be locked away from the world, you just need to speak to the right person.

Just like having a disability, you cannot understand something you have never been through yourself.

Seek help, keep going. As much as you feel alone and the world doesn't care, it does.

It took a lot of appointments with different counsellors and psychologists, but I eventually found the right one. You will too, but don't give up.

Just like finding the right relationship with someone, you need to find the right professional. But I implore you, don't give up.

The world is a wonderful place when you clear away depression.

While we focus on other people's lives, we forget about our own....

Scott Healy

Letter To All The Beautiful Souls In The World

I read so many things about people looking for awakenings and enlightenment.

Asking for ways to find things. Looking for things that they are not ready to receive, or may never be able to receive in this lifetime.

There are some levels that take many lifetimes.

I don't doubt that every person has a way of connecting with themselves on a highly spiritual level. But what the level is, depends on what your higher self wants to give you.

The more patient you are, the easier it is to receive.

I was 45 before the spirituality light bulb went on. But I didn't search for it. It found me. It was always there, I was just oblivious to it.

I then started asking questions about myself. Not too deeply, just myself as a human being, and how I could find what I wanted in life.

I didn't meditate. I haven't read self-help books.

I observe people.
I listen to people.
That is the best awakening you can have.

The best enlightenment is listening to yourself, and instead of just being positive to the people around you, be positive to yourself.

Try to find a positive in every negative. Even if it is something small. That small positive outweighs the negative almost every time.

When you start to see positives in a negative, then I promise you that eventually your mind will do it automatically. It might take a short time, it might take a long time, but you will get there.

I personally have never looked for anything spiritual. Things just seem to come along and I go with the flow.

They happen at unexpected times.

Don't ask your higher self to give you gifts of life. Trust your higher self to give you what you need when you need it. Let it happen if it is meant to happen.

Talk to yourself kindly. You are your best friend.

Spirituality is not about religion

*It is about how much your spirit grows
and begins to forgive itself...*

Scott Healy

Passion

Sometimes people confuse passion and anger, especially when it comes to empaths. There is so much passion, so much happiness to give, so much healing to be done for others.

When you are truly happy inside yourself, despite others doubting you, you can then make a difference.

Not all empaths reach a level that they are meant to reach. The burden of life is often too heavy for some.

Being an empath is not always about absorbing pain from other people. It is a journey of self-discovery. A journey that not only teaches you about yourself, but it is a journey that helps you listen. Not to be judgmental, and realise that there are different journeys for everyone.

The more you listen to other people's journeys, the more yours is enriched.

Solitude can be the most blissful for me. It gives me a chance to breathe. Self-reflect. Analyse. Learn. Improve.

"I am no better than anyone.... No one is better than me"

9 780646 820644